# 50 Poland Sandwich Recipes for Home

By: Kelly Johnson

# Table of Contents

- Ziemniaczane Krokiety (Potato Croquettes)
- Kabanosy (Polish Sausages)
- Schabowy Sandwich (Pork Cutlet Sandwich)
- Kanapka z Żółtym Serem (Cheese Sandwich)
- Pastrami z Ogórkiem (Pastrami with Pickles)
- Śledź w Śmietanie (Herring in Cream)
- Kanapka z Sałatką Jajeczną (Egg Salad Sandwich)
- Polskie Kiełbasy (Polish Sausages)
- Pstrąg w Bułce (Trout Sandwich)
- Kanapka z Kurczakiem (Chicken Sandwich)
- Placki Ziemniaczane (Potato Pancakes)
- Kanapka z Kiełbasą (Sausage Sandwich)
- Kiełbasa Wiejska (Country Sausage)
- Klopsiki (Meatballs)
- Kanapka z Sernikiem (Cheese Sandwich)
- Żurek z Chlebem (Sour Rye Soup with Bread)
- Kanapka z Pstrągiem (Trout Sandwich)
- Kanapka z Gulaszem (Goulash Sandwich)
- Kotlet Mielony (Minced Meat Cutlet)
- Kanapka z Ogórkiem (Cucumber Sandwich)
- Pasztet (Liver Pâté)
- Kanapka z Szynką (Ham Sandwich)
- Kiełbasa w Cebuli (Sausage with Onion)
- Kanapka z Boczniakiem (Oyster Mushroom Sandwich)
- Jajecznica na Chlebie (Scrambled Eggs on Bread)
- Kanapka z Wędliną (Cold Cuts Sandwich)
- Żurek z Kiełbasą (Sour Rye Soup with Sausage)
- Kanapka z Sałatką (Salad Sandwich)
- Kiełbasa w Musztardzie (Sausage with Mustard)
- Kanapka z Pstrągiem w Sosie (Trout Sandwich in Sauce)
- Kotlet Po Wiedeńsku (Viennese Cutlet)
- Kanapka z Rillettes (Pork Rillettes Sandwich)

- Schab po Warszawsku (Warsaw-style Pork)
- Kanapka z Kapustą (Cabbage Sandwich)
- Sernik na Zimno (Cold Cheesecake)
- Kanapka z Wątróbką (Liver Sandwich)
- Placki z Kurczaka (Chicken Pancakes)
- Kanapka z Krewetkami (Shrimp Sandwich)
- Zupa Pomidorowa z Chlebem (Tomato Soup with Bread)
- Kanapka z Pstrągiem w Bułce (Trout in Bread)
- Kotlet w Bułce (Cutlet in Bread)
- Kanapka z Tuńczykiem (Tuna Sandwich)
- Ziemniaki z Boczkiem (Potatoes with Bacon)
- Kanapka z Mieszanką Wędlin (Mixed Cold Cuts Sandwich)
- Schab z Kością (Bone-in Pork Cutlet)
- Kanapka z Kiełbasą Wieprzową (Pork Sausage Sandwich)
- Wątróbka w Śmietanie (Liver in Cream)
- Kanapka z Pieczonym Kurczakiem (Roast Chicken Sandwich)
- Placki Ziemniaczane z Wędliną (Potato Pancakes with Cold Cuts)
- Kanapka z Fasolką (Bean Sandwich)

**Ziemniaczane Krokiety (Potato Croquettes)**

**Ingredients:**

- 4 medium potatoes
- 1 small onion, finely chopped
- 1 egg
- 1 cup bread crumbs
- 1/2 cup grated cheese (optional)
- 2 tbsp chopped fresh parsley
- Salt and pepper to taste
- Oil for frying

**Instructions:**

1. **Prepare Potatoes:**
    - Peel and cut the potatoes into chunks. Boil in salted water until tender, about 15-20 minutes. Drain and mash until smooth.
2. **Prepare Filling:**
    - In a skillet, sauté the chopped onion in a bit of oil until golden and softened. Add to the mashed potatoes.
3. **Mix Ingredients:**
    - To the mashed potatoes and onions, add the egg, bread crumbs, grated cheese (if using), and parsley. Season with salt and pepper. Mix well until the mixture holds together.
4. **Shape Croquettes:**
    - Shape the mixture into small oval or round patties.
5. **Coat Croquettes:**
    - Roll each croquette in additional bread crumbs to coat evenly.
6. **Fry Croquettes:**
    - Heat oil in a frying pan over medium heat. Fry the croquettes in batches, turning occasionally, until golden brown and crispy, about 3-4 minutes per side.
7. **Drain and Serve:**
    - Remove from oil and drain on paper towels. Serve warm.

These croquettes can be served as a side dish or used as a filling for sandwiches. Enjoy!

# Kabanosy (Polish Sausages)

## Ingredients:

- 2 lbs (900 g) pork shoulder or pork butt, cut into chunks
- 1/2 lb (225 g) beef chuck, cut into chunks
- 1/2 cup (120 ml) cold water
- 2 tsp salt
- 1 tsp black pepper
- 1 tsp paprika (sweet or smoked)
- 1/2 tsp garlic powder
- 1/2 tsp caraway seeds (optional)
- 1/2 tsp dried marjoram (optional)
- 1/4 tsp curing salt (Prague Powder #1) (optional, for preservation)
- 1/4 cup (60 ml) white wine (optional)
- Sausage casings (hog casings or collagen casings, soaked and rinsed if necessary)

## Instructions:

1. **Prepare the Meat:**
   - Grind the pork and beef through a medium-hole grinder. You can use a food processor if you don't have a grinder, but ensure the mixture remains cold.
2. **Mix Ingredients:**
   - In a large bowl, combine the ground meats with salt, black pepper, paprika, garlic powder, caraway seeds, marjoram, and curing salt if using. Add cold water and white wine (if using), and mix thoroughly until the mixture is sticky and well combined.
3. **Prepare the Casings:**
   - If using natural casings, rinse them thoroughly under cold water and soak them in water for about 30 minutes. Rinse again and keep them in fresh water until you're ready to stuff them. If using collagen casings, follow the package instructions.
4. **Stuff the Sausages:**
   - Fit your sausage stuffer with the casings and slide them onto the stuffer's tube. Tie a knot at the end of the casing. Stuff the casing with the sausage mixture, being careful not to overstuff. Twist the sausages into 12-15 inch links and tie off the open end.
5. **Cure and Dry:**
   - Hang the sausages in a cool, dry place or in a refrigerator with good airflow to cure. They should be dried for about 3-5 days. The drying time can vary depending on humidity and temperature.
6. **Cook or Store:**

- Once dried, kabanosy can be eaten as is or cooked. To cook, grill or pan-fry until heated through and slightly crispy. If not eating immediately, store them in an airtight container or vacuum-sealed bag.

Enjoy your homemade kabanosy in sandwiches, as a snack, or as part of a Polish-themed meal!

# Schabowy Sandwich (Pork Cutlet Sandwich)

**Ingredients:**

- **For the Pork Cutlets:**
    - 4 boneless pork chops or pork loin steaks (about 1/2 inch thick)
    - 1 cup all-purpose flour
    - 2 large eggs
    - 1 cup bread crumbs (preferably panko for extra crunch)
    - Salt and pepper to taste
    - 1 tsp paprika (optional)
    - Vegetable oil for frying
- **For the Sandwich:**
    - 4 sandwich rolls or crusty bread rolls
    - 4 tbsp mayonnaise or mustard (optional)
    - Lettuce leaves
    - Tomato slices
    - Pickles or cucumber slices
    - Sliced red onion (optional)

**Instructions:**

1. **Prepare the Pork Cutlets:**
    - Place the pork chops between two sheets of plastic wrap or parchment paper. Use a meat mallet or rolling pin to pound them to an even thickness of about 1/4 inch.
    - Season both sides of the pork cutlets with salt, pepper, and paprika if using.
2. **Bread the Cutlets:**
    - Set up a breading station: Place flour in one shallow dish, beat eggs in a second dish, and place bread crumbs in a third dish.
    - Dredge each pork cutlet in flour, shaking off excess. Dip in beaten eggs, allowing excess to drip off. Coat thoroughly with bread crumbs, pressing them in gently to adhere.
3. **Fry the Cutlets:**
    - Heat vegetable oil in a large skillet over medium heat. You need enough oil to cover the bottom of the skillet.
    - Fry the pork cutlets for 3-4 minutes per side, or until golden brown and cooked through. Transfer to a paper towel-lined plate to drain excess oil.
4. **Assemble the Sandwich:**
    - If desired, lightly toast the sandwich rolls.
    - Spread mayonnaise or mustard on the inside of the rolls if using.
    - Place a pork cutlet on the bottom half of each roll.

- Top with lettuce, tomato slices, pickles or cucumber slices, and red onion if desired.
- Place the top half of the roll on the sandwich and serve immediately.

## Serving Suggestions:

- Serve with a side of coleslaw, potato salad, or pickled vegetables.
- Pair with a light, crisp salad or enjoy it with a cold beverage.

Enjoy your Schabowy Sandwich! It's a classic Polish comfort food that's sure to satisfy your taste buds.

**Kanapka z Żółtym Serem (Cheese Sandwich)**

**Ingredients:**

- 2 slices of bread (white, rye, or whole wheat)
- 2-3 slices of yellow cheese (like Edam, Gouda, or Swiss)
- 1-2 tbsp butter or margarine
- 1-2 lettuce leaves (optional)
- 1 tomato, sliced (optional)
- Pickles or cucumber slices (optional)
- Salt and pepper to taste

**Instructions:**

1. **Prepare the Bread:**
   - Spread butter or margarine evenly on one side of each slice of bread.
2. **Assemble the Sandwich:**
   - Place the cheese slices on the unbuttered side of one slice of bread.
   - If desired, add lettuce, tomato slices, pickles, or cucumber on top of the cheese.
   - Season with a pinch of salt and pepper if desired.
3. **Finish the Sandwich:**
   - Top with the second slice of bread, buttered side facing up.
4. **Optional: Toast the Sandwich:**
   - For a warm, crispy sandwich, toast it in a skillet over medium heat or use a sandwich press until the bread is golden brown and the cheese is melted.

## Serving Suggestions:

- Serve with a side salad, soup, or some fresh fruit for a complete meal.
- You can also add ham or turkey for extra protein if you like.

Enjoy your Kanapka z Żółtym Serem!

**Pastrami z Ogórkiem (Pastrami with Pickles)**

**Ingredients:**

- 2 slices of rye bread or your preferred sandwich bread
- 4-6 slices of pastrami
- 1-2 dill pickles, sliced
- 1-2 tbsp mustard (optional)
- 1-2 lettuce leaves (optional)
- 1 slice of cheese (optional)
- Salt and pepper to taste

**Instructions:**

1. **Prepare the Bread:**
   - If desired, lightly toast the bread slices.
2. **Assemble the Sandwich:**
   - Spread mustard on one or both slices of bread if using.
   - Layer pastrami evenly over one slice of bread.
   - Add pickle slices on top of the pastrami.
   - Optionally, add lettuce and cheese.
3. **Season and Close:**
   - Season with a pinch of salt and pepper if desired.
   - Top with the second slice of bread.

## Serving Suggestions:

- Serve with a side of coleslaw, potato chips, or a simple salad.
- For added flavor, you can also add a layer of sauerkraut or a slice of tomato.

Enjoy your Pastrami z Ogórkiem!

**Śledź w Śmietanie (Herring in Cream)**

**Ingredients:**

- 1 jar (about 12 oz or 340 g) pickled herring fillets (such as Matjes herring)
- 1 cup (240 ml) sour cream
- 1/2 cup (120 ml) heavy cream
- 1 small onion, finely chopped
- 1 apple, peeled, cored, and diced
- 1-2 tbsp white wine vinegar or lemon juice (to taste)
- 1-2 tbsp chopped fresh dill or parsley
- Salt and pepper to taste

**Instructions:**

1. **Prepare the Herring:**
   - Drain the pickled herring fillets and rinse them under cold water to remove excess brine. Pat dry with paper towels.
   - Cut the herring fillets into bite-sized pieces.
2. **Prepare the Cream Mixture:**
   - In a bowl, combine the sour cream and heavy cream. Stir until smooth.
   - Add the finely chopped onion, diced apple, and chopped dill or parsley. Mix well.
   - Season with white wine vinegar or lemon juice, salt, and pepper to taste.
3. **Combine Ingredients:**
   - Gently fold the herring pieces into the cream mixture, ensuring they are well coated.
4. **Chill:**
   - Cover the bowl and refrigerate for at least 1 hour before serving to allow the flavors to meld.
5. **Serve:**
   - Serve the Śledź w Śmietanie chilled, garnished with additional dill or parsley if desired. It's typically enjoyed with rye bread, boiled potatoes, or as part of a cold appetizer platter.

## Serving Suggestions:

- Serve with boiled potatoes, rye bread, or as part of a larger spread with other Polish dishes.
- It pairs well with a crisp, dry white wine or a cold beer.

Enjoy your Śledź w Śmietanie! It's a delightful combination of creamy, tangy, and savory flavors that capture the essence of Polish cuisine.

**Kanapka z Sałatką Jajeczną (Egg Salad Sandwich)**

**Ingredients:**

- 4 large eggs
- 2-3 tbsp mayonnaise
- 1 tsp Dijon mustard (optional)
- 1-2 tbsp finely chopped fresh chives or parsley
- Salt and pepper to taste
- 4 slices of bread (white, rye, or whole wheat)
- Lettuce leaves (optional)
- Sliced cucumber or tomato (optional)

**Instructions:**

1. **Prepare the Eggs:**
    - Place the eggs in a pot and cover with cold water. Bring to a boil over medium-high heat. Once boiling, reduce heat and simmer for 10 minutes.
    - Remove the eggs and place them in a bowl of ice water to cool. Peel and chop the eggs into small pieces.
2. **Make the Egg Salad:**
    - In a bowl, combine the chopped eggs, mayonnaise, and Dijon mustard if using. Mix until well combined.
    - Add the chopped chives or parsley. Season with salt and pepper to taste. Mix well.
3. **Assemble the Sandwich:**
    - If desired, spread a thin layer of butter or additional mayonnaise on the bread slices.
    - Spoon the egg salad mixture onto one slice of bread.
    - Add lettuce leaves and cucumber or tomato slices if desired.
    - Top with the second slice of bread.
4. **Serve:**
    - Cut the sandwich into halves or quarters if desired and serve immediately.

## Serving Suggestions:

- Pair with a simple green salad, some pickles, or a piece of fresh fruit.
- For added texture, you can toast the bread before assembling the sandwich.

Enjoy your Kanapka z Sałatką Jajeczną! It's a classic and comforting choice that's both easy to prepare and satisfying.

**Polskie Kiełbasy (Polish Sausages)**

**Ingredients:**

- **For the Sausage Mix:**
    - 2 lbs (900 g) pork shoulder or pork butt, cut into chunks
    - 1/2 lb (225 g) beef chuck or veal (optional), cut into chunks
    - 1/2 cup (120 ml) cold water
    - 2 tsp salt
    - 1 tsp black pepper
    - 1 tsp paprika (sweet or smoked)
    - 1/2 tsp garlic powder
    - 1/2 tsp caraway seeds (optional)
    - 1/2 tsp dried marjoram
    - 1/4 tsp curing salt (Prague Powder #1) (optional, for preservation)
    - 1/4 cup (60 ml) white wine or beer (optional)
    - Sausage casings (hog casings or collagen casings, soaked and rinsed if necessary)

**Instructions:**

1. **Prepare the Meat:**
    - Grind the pork (and beef or veal, if using) through a medium-hole grinder. For a finer texture, you can grind the meat twice.
2. **Mix the Ingredients:**
    - In a large bowl, combine the ground meat with salt, black pepper, paprika, garlic powder, caraway seeds, marjoram, and curing salt if using.
    - Add cold water and white wine or beer (if using) and mix thoroughly until the mixture is sticky and well combined.
3. **Prepare the Casings:**
    - If using natural casings, rinse them thoroughly under cold water and soak them in water for about 30 minutes. Rinse again and keep them in fresh water until you're ready to stuff them. If using collagen casings, follow the package instructions.
4. **Stuff the Sausages:**
    - Fit your sausage stuffer with the casings and slide them onto the stuffer's tube. Tie a knot at the end of the casing. Stuff the casing with the sausage mixture, being careful not to overstuff. Twist sausages into 12-15 inch links and tie off the open end.
5. **Cure and Dry:**
    - Hang the sausages in a cool, dry place or in a refrigerator with good airflow to cure. They should be dried for about 3-5 days. The drying time can vary depending on humidity and temperature.
6. **Cook or Store:**

- Once dried, Polish sausages can be eaten as is or cooked. To cook, grill, pan-fry, or bake until heated through and slightly crispy. If not eating immediately, store them in an airtight container or vacuum-sealed bag.

**Serving Suggestions:**

- Enjoy the sausages with sauerkraut, mustard, and fresh bread.
- Serve them as part of a Polish-themed meal with potatoes, pickles, or a side of vegetables.
- They can also be sliced and added to soups, stews, or casseroles.

Enjoy making and tasting your homemade Polskie Kiełbasy! They're a flavorful addition to any meal and a true taste of Polish tradition.

**Pstrąg w Bułce (Trout Sandwich)**

**Ingredients:**

- 2 fresh trout fillets (or 1 whole trout, cleaned and deboned)
- 2 tbsp flour
- 1 egg, beaten
- 1 cup bread crumbs
- Salt and pepper to taste
- 2 tbsp olive oil or butter
- 2 sandwich rolls or crusty bread rolls
- 1 tbsp mayonnaise (optional)
- Lettuce leaves
- Tomato slices
- Lemon wedges (for garnish)
- Fresh dill (optional, for garnish)

**Instructions:**

1. **Prepare the Trout:**
   - Season the trout fillets with salt and pepper.
   - Dredge each fillet in flour, shaking off excess. Dip in beaten egg, then coat with bread crumbs.
2. **Cook the Trout:**
   - Heat olive oil or butter in a skillet over medium heat.
   - Fry the trout fillets for 3-4 minutes per side, or until golden brown and cooked through. Alternatively, you can grill the fillets.
3. **Assemble the Sandwich:**
   - If desired, lightly toast the sandwich rolls.
   - Spread mayonnaise on the inside of the rolls if using.
   - Place the cooked trout fillet on the bottom half of each roll.
   - Top with lettuce leaves and tomato slices.
4. **Serve:**
   - Garnish with a lemon wedge and fresh dill if desired.
   - Serve immediately.

## Serving Suggestions:

- Enjoy with a side salad, potato wedges, or pickles.
- Pair with a crisp white wine or a light beer.

Enjoy your Pstrąg w Bułce! It's a fresh and flavorful sandwich that's easy to prepare and perfect for a quick lunch or dinner.

**Kanapka z Kurczakiem (Chicken Sandwich)**

**Ingredients:**

- 2 cups cooked chicken, shredded or sliced (e.g., from a roasted or grilled chicken breast)
- 2 tbsp mayonnaise
- 1 tbsp Dijon mustard (optional)
- 1 tbsp lemon juice or vinegar
- 1-2 celery stalks, finely chopped
- 1/4 cup red onion, finely chopped
- 2 tbsp fresh parsley or dill, chopped (optional)
- Salt and pepper to taste
- 4 slices of bread (white, whole wheat, or rye) or 2 sandwich rolls
- Lettuce leaves
- Tomato slices (optional)
- Pickles or cucumber slices (optional)

**Instructions:**

1. **Prepare the Chicken Salad:**
   - In a large bowl, combine the shredded or sliced chicken with mayonnaise, Dijon mustard (if using), and lemon juice or vinegar.
   - Add the finely chopped celery, red onion, and fresh herbs if desired.
   - Mix well and season with salt and pepper to taste.
2. **Assemble the Sandwich:**
   - If desired, toast the bread slices or sandwich rolls.
   - Spread the chicken salad evenly on one slice of bread or on the bottom half of each sandwich roll.
   - Top with lettuce leaves and tomato slices if using.
   - Add pickles or cucumber slices if desired.
   - Place the second slice of bread on top or the top half of the roll.
3. **Serve:**
   - Cut the sandwich in half if desired and serve immediately.

## Serving Suggestions:

- Serve with a side of chips, a simple green salad, or fresh fruit.
- For added flavor, you can add a slice of cheese or avocado to the sandwich.

Enjoy your Kanapka z Kurczakiem! It's a tasty and customizable sandwich that's perfect for lunch or a quick meal.

**Placki Ziemniaczane (Potato Pancakes)**

**Ingredients:**

- 4 large potatoes, peeled
- 1 small onion
- 1 large egg
- 1/4 cup all-purpose flour
- Salt and pepper to taste
- Vegetable oil for frying
- Sour cream or applesauce for serving (optional)

**Instructions:**

1. **Prepare the Potatoes:**
    - Grate the potatoes using a box grater or food processor. Place the grated potatoes in a clean kitchen towel and squeeze out excess moisture.
2. **Prepare the Onion:**
    - Grate the onion and mix it with the grated potatoes.
3. **Make the Batter:**
    - In a large bowl, combine the grated potatoes and onion with the egg, flour, salt, and pepper. Mix well until the mixture holds together.
4. **Fry the Pancakes:**
    - Heat a generous amount of vegetable oil in a skillet over medium-high heat.
    - Spoon tablespoons of the potato mixture into the hot oil, flattening them with the back of the spoon to form pancakes.
    - Fry for 3-4 minutes on each side, or until golden brown and crispy. Transfer to a paper towel-lined plate to drain excess oil.
5. **Serve:**
    - Serve hot with sour cream or applesauce if desired.

## Serving Suggestions:

- Enjoy as a side dish or main course with a dollop of sour cream or applesauce.
- Can also be served with a side of sautéed mushrooms or a simple salad.

Enjoy your Placki Ziemniaczane! They're a comforting and satisfying treat that's sure to please.

**Kanapka z Kiełbasą (Sausage Sandwich)**

**Ingredients:**

- 2 Polish sausages (like kiełbasa or bratwurst)
- 2 sandwich rolls or crusty bread rolls
- 1 tbsp mustard (optional)
- 1 tbsp mayonnaise (optional)
- Sauerkraut or pickled vegetables (optional)
- 1 onion, thinly sliced
- 1-2 tbsp vegetable oil (for frying the sausage)
- Salt and pepper to taste
- Fresh parsley or dill (for garnish, optional)

**Instructions:**

1. **Cook the Sausages:**
   - Heat vegetable oil in a skillet over medium heat.
   - Cook the sausages for about 5-7 minutes, turning occasionally, until browned and cooked through. Alternatively, you can grill the sausages.
2. **Prepare the Onions:**
   - In the same skillet, sauté the thinly sliced onions until they are golden and caramelized, about 5-7 minutes.
3. **Assemble the Sandwich:**
   - If desired, lightly toast the sandwich rolls.
   - Spread mustard and/or mayonnaise on the inside of each roll if using.
   - Place the cooked sausage on the bottom half of each roll.
   - Top with sautéed onions and sauerkraut or pickled vegetables if desired.
   - Garnish with fresh parsley or dill if using.
4. **Serve:**
   - Close the sandwich with the top half of the roll and serve immediately.

## Serving Suggestions:

- Enjoy with a side of potato salad, chips, or a fresh green salad.
- Pair with a cold beer or a crisp, light beverage.

Enjoy your Kanapka z Kiełbasą! It's a satisfying and flavorful sandwich that's perfect for lunch or a casual meal.

**Kiełbasa Wiejska (Country Sausage)**

**Ingredients:**

- 2 lbs (900 g) pork shoulder or pork butt, cut into chunks
- 1/2 lb (225 g) pork belly, cut into chunks (for added fat and flavor)
- 1/2 cup (120 ml) cold water
- 4 cloves garlic, minced
- 1 tbsp salt
- 1 tsp black pepper
- 1 tsp dried marjoram
- 1/2 tsp paprika (sweet or smoked)
- 1/4 tsp caraway seeds (optional)
- 1/4 tsp curing salt (Prague Powder #1) (optional, for preservation)
- Sausage casings (hog casings or collagen casings, soaked and rinsed if necessary)

**Instructions:**

1. **Prepare the Meat:**
    - Grind the pork shoulder and pork belly through a medium-hole grinder. For a finer texture, you can grind the meat twice.
2. **Mix the Ingredients:**
    - In a large bowl, combine the ground meat with minced garlic, salt, black pepper, marjoram, paprika, caraway seeds (if using), and curing salt if using.
    - Add the cold water and mix thoroughly until the mixture is sticky and well combined.
3. **Prepare the Casings:**
    - If using natural casings, rinse them thoroughly under cold water and soak them in water for about 30 minutes. Rinse again and keep them in fresh water until you're ready to stuff them. If using collagen casings, follow the package instructions.
4. **Stuff the Sausages:**
    - Fit your sausage stuffer with the casings and slide them onto the stuffer's tube. Tie a knot at the end of the casing.
    - Stuff the casing with the sausage mixture, being careful not to overstuff. Twist sausages into 12-15 inch links and tie off the open end.
5. **Cure and Dry:**
    - Hang the sausages in a cool, dry place or in a refrigerator with good airflow to cure. They should be dried for about 3-5 days. The drying time can vary depending on humidity and temperature.
6. **Cook or Store:**
    - Once dried, Kiełbasa Wiejska can be cooked by grilling, pan-frying, or baking until heated through. If not eating immediately, store the sausages in an airtight container or vacuum-sealed bag.

## Serving Suggestions:

- Serve Kiełbasa Wiejska with sauerkraut, mustard, and fresh bread.
- It can also be used in soups, stews, or as part of a charcuterie board.

Enjoy making and tasting your homemade Kiełbasa Wiejska! It's a flavorful and satisfying sausage that reflects the rich tradition of Polish cuisine.

**Klopsiki (Meatballs)**

**Ingredients:**

- 1 lb (450 g) ground beef
- 1/2 lb (225 g) ground pork (or use all beef if preferred)
- 1 small onion, finely chopped
- 1 slice of bread, soaked in 1/4 cup (60 ml) milk
- 1 large egg
- 2 cloves garlic, minced
- 1 tsp dried marjoram
- 1/2 tsp paprika
- Salt and pepper to taste
- 2 tbsp vegetable oil (for frying)

**Instructions:**

1. **Prepare the Bread:**
   - Soak the bread slice in milk until soft, then squeeze out excess liquid and crumble the bread into small pieces.
2. **Mix the Meat:**
   - In a large bowl, combine the ground beef and pork, chopped onion, crumbled bread, egg, minced garlic, dried marjoram, paprika, salt, and pepper. Mix until well combined but avoid overmixing to keep the meatballs tender.
3. **Shape the Meatballs:**
   - Form the mixture into meatballs, about 1-1.5 inches in diameter.
4. **Cook the Meatballs:**
   - Heat vegetable oil in a large skillet over medium heat.
   - Fry the meatballs in batches, turning occasionally, until browned on all sides and cooked through, about 10-15 minutes. You can also bake them at 375°F (190°C) for 20-25 minutes if you prefer less oil.
5. **Serve:**
   - Serve the klopsiki hot with a side of mashed potatoes, rice, or pasta. They can also be served in a tomato sauce or gravy.

## Serving Suggestions:

- Pair with a side of steamed vegetables or a fresh salad.
- For a traditional touch, serve with sauerkraut or pickled cucumbers.

Enjoy your Klopsiki! They're a comforting and versatile dish that's sure to please.

**Kanapka z Sernikiem (Cheese Sandwich)**

**Ingredients:**

- 2 slices of bread (white, whole wheat, or rye)
- 2-3 slices of cheese (e.g., Edam, Gouda, or your favorite cheese)
- 1-2 tbsp butter or margarine
- Lettuce leaves (optional)
- Tomato slices (optional)
- Pickles or cucumber slices (optional)
- Fresh herbs like dill or parsley (optional)

**Instructions:**

1. **Prepare the Bread:**
    - If desired, lightly toast the bread slices.
2. **Assemble the Sandwich:**
    - Spread butter or margarine on one side of each bread slice if using.
    - Layer the cheese slices evenly on one slice of bread.
    - Add lettuce leaves, tomato slices, pickles, or cucumber slices if desired.
3. **Top and Serve:**
    - Place the second slice of bread on top, buttered side facing inward.
    - Slice the sandwich in half if desired.

## Serving Suggestions:

- Serve with a side salad, some fresh fruit, or a few crunchy pickles.
- Pair with a light beverage or a cup of tea.

Enjoy your Kanapka z Sernikiem! It's a versatile and satisfying option for a quick meal or snack.

**Żurek z Chlebem (Sour Rye Soup with Bread)**

**Ingredients:**

- **For the Soup:**
    - 1 cup sour rye starter (żur), or use 2 cups of prepared żurek mix available in stores
    - 1 lb (450 g) smoked sausage or kielbasa, sliced
    - 1 medium onion, chopped
    - 2 cloves garlic, minced
    - 1 bay leaf
    - 1 tsp dried marjoram
    - 1-2 medium potatoes, peeled and diced
    - 4 cups (1 liter) beef or vegetable broth
    - 1 tbsp vegetable oil
    - Salt and pepper to taste
- **For Serving:**
    - 4 round bread rolls (or 1 large round loaf of bread)
    - Fresh parsley or dill, chopped (for garnish)
    - Hard-boiled eggs (optional, for garnish)

**Instructions:**

1. **Prepare the Soup Base:**
    - In a large pot, heat vegetable oil over medium heat. Add chopped onion and cook until softened and translucent, about 5 minutes.
    - Add minced garlic and cook for an additional 1 minute.
2. **Add the Sausage and Potatoes:**
    - Add the sliced sausage to the pot and cook for 5-7 minutes, allowing it to brown slightly.
    - Add diced potatoes, bay leaf, and dried marjoram. Stir to combine.
3. **Add the Broth:**
    - Pour in the beef or vegetable broth and bring to a boil. Reduce heat and simmer until the potatoes are tender, about 10-15 minutes.
4. **Incorporate the Żurek:**
    - Stir in the sour rye starter (żur) or prepared żurek mix. Simmer for an additional 5 minutes. Adjust seasoning with salt and pepper to taste.
5. **Prepare the Bread Bowls:**
    - If using bread rolls, cut off the tops and hollow out the centers to create a bowl. If using a large loaf, cut the top off and hollow out the loaf to create a large bowl.
6. **Serve the Soup:**
    - Ladle the hot soup into the prepared bread bowls.
    - Garnish with chopped parsley or dill and optional hard-boiled eggs.

## Serving Suggestions:

- Serve with extra bread or rye rolls on the side.
- Enjoy with a side of pickles or a fresh green salad.

**Żurek z Chlebem** is a comforting and hearty soup that combines the tanginess of sour rye with the richness of smoked sausage and tender potatoes. Enjoy this traditional Polish dish!

**Kanapka z Pstrągiem (Trout Sandwich)**

**Ingredients:**

- 2 fresh trout fillets (or 1 whole trout, cleaned and deboned)
- 2 tbsp flour
- 1 egg, beaten
- 1 cup breadcrumbs
- Salt and pepper to taste
- 2 tbsp olive oil or butter (for cooking)
- 2 sandwich rolls or slices of crusty bread
- 1 tbsp mayonnaise (optional)
- 1 tbsp Dijon mustard (optional)
- Lettuce leaves
- Tomato slices
- Cucumber slices
- Fresh dill or parsley (optional, for garnish)
- Lemon wedges (for garnish)

**Instructions:**

1. **Prepare the Trout:**
   - Season the trout fillets with salt and pepper.
   - Dredge each fillet in flour, shaking off the excess. Dip in beaten egg, then coat with breadcrumbs.
2. **Cook the Trout:**
   - Heat olive oil or butter in a skillet over medium heat.
   - Fry the trout fillets for 3-4 minutes on each side, or until golden brown and cooked through. Alternatively, you can grill the fillets.
3. **Prepare the Bread:**
   - If desired, lightly toast the sandwich rolls or bread slices.
4. **Assemble the Sandwich:**
   - Spread mayonnaise and/or Dijon mustard on the inside of the bread rolls or slices.
   - Place the cooked trout fillet on the bottom half of each roll or slice of bread.
   - Top with lettuce leaves, tomato slices, and cucumber slices.
5. **Garnish and Serve:**
   - Garnish with fresh dill or parsley if desired.
   - Serve with lemon wedges on the side.

## Serving Suggestions:

- Enjoy the trout sandwich with a side of coleslaw, potato salad, or a simple green salad.
- Pair with a crisp white wine or a light beer.

**Kanapka z Pstrągiem** is a fresh and satisfying sandwich that highlights the delicate flavor of trout. It's perfect for a light lunch or dinner.

**Kanapka z Gulaszem (Goulash Sandwich)**

**Ingredients:**

- **For the Goulash:**
    - 1 lb (450 g) beef stew meat, cut into bite-sized pieces
    - 2 tbsp vegetable oil
    - 1 large onion, chopped
    - 2 cloves garlic, minced
    - 1 red bell pepper, diced
    - 2 tbsp paprika (sweet or smoked)
    - 1 tsp caraway seeds (optional)
    - 1 cup beef broth
    - 1 can (14.5 oz) diced tomatoes
    - 1-2 tbsp tomato paste
    - Salt and pepper to taste
    - 1-2 tsp dried marjoram or thyme (optional)
    - 1-2 tbsp flour (optional, for thickening)
- **For the Sandwich:**
    - 4 sandwich rolls or crusty bread rolls
    - Lettuce or arugula (optional, for garnish)

**Instructions:**

1. **Cook the Goulash:**
    - Heat vegetable oil in a large skillet or pot over medium heat.
    - Add beef pieces and brown on all sides. Remove beef and set aside.
    - In the same pan, add chopped onion and cook until softened, about 5 minutes.
    - Add minced garlic and diced red bell pepper, and cook for another 2 minutes.
    - Stir in paprika and caraway seeds (if using), and cook for 1 minute.
    - Return beef to the pan and add beef broth, diced tomatoes, and tomato paste. Stir well.
    - Bring to a boil, then reduce heat to low and simmer for 1-1.5 hours, or until beef is tender and sauce has thickened. If needed, mix flour with a bit of water and stir into the goulash to thicken.
2. **Prepare the Bread:**
    - If desired, lightly toast the sandwich rolls or bread slices.
3. **Assemble the Sandwich:**
    - Spoon the hot goulash onto the bottom half of each bread roll.
    - Optionally, add lettuce or arugula on top of the goulash.
    - Place the top half of the roll on the sandwich.
4. **Serve:**
    - Serve immediately while the goulash is hot.

# Serving Suggestions:

- Enjoy with a side of pickles or a simple salad.
- Pair with a cold beer or a hearty red wine.

**Kanapka z Gulaszem** offers a flavorful and comforting meal, perfect for a hearty lunch or dinner.

**Kotlet Mielony (Minced Meat Cutlet)**

**Ingredients:**

- 1 lb (450 g) ground beef (or a mix of beef and pork)
- 1 small onion, finely chopped
- 1 egg
- 1 slice of bread, soaked in 1/4 cup (60 ml) milk
- 1/4 cup (30 g) breadcrumbs
- 2 cloves garlic, minced
- 1 tsp dried thyme or marjoram
- Salt and pepper to taste
- 1/2 cup (60 g) breadcrumbs (for coating)
- Vegetable oil for frying

**Instructions:**

1. **Prepare the Meat Mixture:**
   - In a large bowl, combine ground meat, finely chopped onion, egg, soaked and crumbled bread, 1/4 cup breadcrumbs, minced garlic, thyme or marjoram, salt, and pepper. Mix until well combined but do not overmix to keep the cutlets tender.
2. **Shape the Cutlets:**
   - Form the mixture into patties about 1/2 inch thick.
3. **Coat the Cutlets:**
   - Place 1/2 cup of breadcrumbs in a shallow dish. Coat each patty in breadcrumbs, pressing lightly to adhere.
4. **Fry the Cutlets:**
   - Heat vegetable oil in a large skillet over medium heat.
   - Fry the cutlets for 4-5 minutes on each side, or until golden brown and cooked through. Adjust the heat as needed to prevent burning.
5. **Drain and Serve:**
   - Transfer cooked cutlets to a paper towel-lined plate to drain excess oil.

## Serving Suggestions:

- Serve with mashed potatoes, sauerkraut, or a side salad.
- Accompany with a dollop of sour cream or your favorite sauce.

**Kotlet Mielony** is a comforting and flavorful dish that's perfect for a hearty meal. Enjoy!

### Kanapka z Ogórkiem (Cucumber Sandwich)

**Ingredients:**

- 4 slices of bread (white, whole wheat, or rye)
- 1 cucumber, thinly sliced
- 2-3 tbsp cream cheese or butter
- Fresh dill or parsley (optional, for garnish)
- Salt and pepper to taste

**Instructions:**

1. **Prepare the Bread:**
   - If desired, lightly toast the bread slices.
2. **Prepare the Cucumber:**
   - Thinly slice the cucumber. For extra crunch, you can sprinkle the slices with a little salt and let them sit for 5 minutes, then pat dry with paper towels to remove excess moisture.
3. **Assemble the Sandwich:**
   - Spread cream cheese or butter evenly on one side of each bread slice.
   - Arrange cucumber slices on top of the cream cheese or butter.
   - Season with a little salt and pepper.
4. **Garnish and Serve:**
   - Garnish with fresh dill or parsley if desired.
   - Top with another slice of bread to complete the sandwich, then cut into halves or quarters if preferred.

## Serving Suggestions:

- Enjoy with a side of fresh fruit or a simple green salad.
- Pair with a light tea or a refreshing beverage.

**Kanapka z Ogórkiem** is a crisp and cooling sandwich that's perfect for a quick and satisfying bite.

## Pasztet (Liver Pâté)

**Ingredients:**

- 1 lb (450 g) chicken liver (or pork liver)
- 1 small onion, finely chopped
- 2 cloves garlic, minced
- 2 tbsp butter
- 1/4 cup (60 ml) heavy cream
- 1/4 cup (60 ml) chicken or beef broth
- 1/4 tsp dried thyme
- 1/4 tsp dried marjoram
- 1/4 tsp ground nutmeg
- Salt and pepper to taste
- 1 egg, beaten
- 1/4 cup (30 g) breadcrumbs (optional, for a smoother texture)

**Instructions:**

1. **Cook the Liver:**
   - Rinse the liver and remove any connective tissue or fat. Pat dry with paper towels.
   - In a skillet, melt butter over medium heat. Add chopped onion and cook until translucent, about 5 minutes.
   - Add minced garlic and cook for an additional minute.
   - Add the liver and cook until browned and cooked through, about 5-7 minutes, stirring occasionally.
2. **Blend the Mixture:**
   - Transfer the cooked liver and onion mixture to a food processor. Add heavy cream, chicken or beef broth, dried thyme, marjoram, nutmeg, salt, and pepper.
   - Blend until smooth. If desired, mix in breadcrumbs for a smoother texture.
3. **Bake the Pâté:**
   - Preheat your oven to 350°F (175°C).
   - Transfer the pâté mixture to a loaf pan or pâté dish. Smooth the top and brush with beaten egg if desired for a glossy finish.
   - Place the loaf pan in a larger baking dish filled with hot water (a water bath) to prevent the pâté from drying out.
   - Bake for 30-40 minutes, or until set and firm.
4. **Cool and Serve:**
   - Allow the pâté to cool to room temperature, then refrigerate for at least 2 hours or overnight to develop flavors.
   - Serve chilled with crusty bread, crackers, or fresh vegetables.

# Serving Suggestions:

- Garnish with fresh herbs or pickles for added flavor.
- Enjoy with a side of mustard or fruit preserves.

**Pasztet** is a delicious and versatile spread that's perfect for special occasions or everyday meals. Enjoy!

**Kanapka z Szynką (Ham Sandwich)**

**Ingredients:**

- 2 slices of bread (white, whole wheat, or rye)
- 2-3 slices of ham (such as Polish ham, or your favorite type)
- 1-2 tbsp butter or mayonnaise
- 1-2 leaves of lettuce
- 2-3 tomato slices
- 1-2 pickle slices (optional)
- Fresh herbs like dill or parsley (optional, for garnish)

**Instructions:**

1. **Prepare the Bread:**
   - If desired, lightly toast the bread slices.
2. **Spread the Condiments:**
   - Spread butter or mayonnaise evenly on one side of each bread slice.
3. **Assemble the Sandwich:**
   - Place the ham slices on one slice of bread.
   - Add lettuce leaves, tomato slices, and pickle slices if using.
4. **Top and Serve:**
   - Place the second slice of bread on top, condiment side facing the filling.
   - Garnish with fresh herbs if desired, then cut the sandwich in half if preferred.

## Serving Suggestions:

- Enjoy with a side of fresh fruit, chips, or a simple green salad.
- Pair with a light beverage or a cup of tea.

**Kanapka z Szynką** is a classic, satisfying sandwich that's perfect for a quick lunch or snack.

**Kiełbasa w Cebuli (Sausage with Onion)**

**Ingredients:**

- 1 lb (450 g) Polish sausage (kielbasa) or any preferred sausage
- 2 large onions, thinly sliced
- 2 tbsp vegetable oil or butter
- 1 tsp dried thyme or caraway seeds (optional)
- Salt and pepper to taste
- 1/4 cup (60 ml) beer or white wine (optional, for extra flavor)
- Fresh parsley or dill (for garnish, optional)

**Instructions:**

1. **Cook the Sausages:**
   - Slice the sausages into bite-sized pieces.
   - Heat vegetable oil or butter in a large skillet over medium heat.
   - Add sausage pieces and cook until browned on all sides, about 5-7 minutes. Remove and set aside.
2. **Caramelize the Onions:**
   - In the same skillet, add more oil or butter if needed.
   - Add sliced onions and cook over medium-low heat, stirring occasionally, until golden brown and caramelized, about 15-20 minutes.
3. **Combine and Simmer:**
   - Return the sausage pieces to the skillet with the onions.
   - If using, pour in the beer or white wine, and stir to combine.
   - Cook for an additional 5 minutes, allowing flavors to meld and the liquid to reduce slightly.
   - Season with salt, pepper, and dried thyme or caraway seeds if using.
4. **Serve:**
   - Garnish with fresh parsley or dill if desired.
   - Serve hot with crusty bread, mashed potatoes, or a side of sauerkraut.

## Serving Suggestions:

- Pair with a side of pickles or a simple green salad.
- Enjoy with a cold beer or a light beverage.

**Kiełbasa w Cebuli** is a savory and comforting dish that highlights the rich flavors of sausage and sweet onions.

**Kanapka z Boczniakiem (Oyster Mushroom Sandwich)**

**Ingredients:**

- 2 slices of bread (white, whole wheat, or rye)
- 1 cup oyster mushrooms, cleaned and sliced
- 2 tbsp olive oil or butter
- 1 clove garlic, minced
- 1 small onion, finely chopped
- Salt and pepper to taste
- 1 tbsp soy sauce (optional, for extra flavor)
- 1-2 tbsp mayonnaise or cream cheese (optional)
- Lettuce or spinach leaves
- Tomato slices (optional)
- Fresh herbs like parsley or dill (optional, for garnish)

**Instructions:**

1. **Cook the Mushrooms:**
   - Heat olive oil or butter in a skillet over medium heat.
   - Add chopped onion and cook until translucent, about 5 minutes.
   - Add garlic and sliced mushrooms. Cook, stirring occasionally, until mushrooms are tender and golden brown, about 7-10 minutes.
   - Season with salt, pepper, and soy sauce if using.
2. **Prepare the Bread:**
   - If desired, lightly toast the bread slices.
3. **Assemble the Sandwich:**
   - Spread mayonnaise or cream cheese on one side of each bread slice if using.
   - Layer the cooked mushrooms and onions on one slice of bread.
   - Add lettuce or spinach leaves, and tomato slices if desired.
4. **Top and Serve:**
   - Place the second slice of bread on top.
   - Garnish with fresh herbs if desired, then cut the sandwich in half if preferred.

## Serving Suggestions:

- Serve with a side of fresh fruit or a simple salad.
- Pair with a light tea or a refreshing beverage.

**Kanapka z Boczniakiem** offers a delicious, meaty texture and rich flavor, making it a satisfying vegetarian option. Enjoy!

**Jajecznica na Chlebie (Scrambled Eggs on Bread)**

**Ingredients:**

- 2 large eggs
- 2 slices of bread (white, whole wheat, or rye)
- 1 tbsp butter or oil
- Salt and pepper to taste
- Optional: 2 tbsp milk or cream (for creamier eggs)
- Optional: Chopped fresh herbs (e.g., chives, parsley)
- Optional: Grated cheese, diced ham, or sautéed vegetables

**Instructions:**

1. **Prepare the Eggs:**
   - In a bowl, whisk the eggs with salt, pepper, and milk or cream if using.
2. **Cook the Eggs:**
   - Heat butter or oil in a non-stick skillet over medium-low heat.
   - Pour in the egg mixture and cook, stirring gently with a spatula, until the eggs are softly scrambled and cooked through. Remove from heat.
3. **Prepare the Bread:**
   - Toast the bread slices if desired.
4. **Assemble the Dish:**
   - Place the scrambled eggs on top of the toasted bread slices.
   - Garnish with chopped fresh herbs, grated cheese, or additional toppings if desired.

## Serving Suggestions:

- Serve with a side of fresh fruit or a light salad.
- Pair with a hot cup of coffee or tea.

**Jajecznica na Chlebie** is a comforting and versatile dish that makes for a quick and satisfying meal. Enjoy!

**Kanapka z Wędliną (Cold Cuts Sandwich)**

**Ingredients:**

- 2 slices of bread (white, whole wheat, or rye)
- 3-4 slices of cold cuts (e.g., ham, salami, turkey, or roast beef)
- 1-2 tbsp mayonnaise, mustard, or butter
- Lettuce leaves
- Tomato slices
- Cucumber slices
- Pickles or gherkins (optional)
- Fresh herbs like parsley or dill (optional)

**Instructions:**

1. **Prepare the Bread:**
   - If desired, lightly toast the bread slices.
2. **Spread Condiments:**
   - Spread mayonnaise, mustard, or butter on one side of each bread slice.
3. **Assemble the Sandwich:**
   - Layer cold cuts evenly on one slice of bread.
   - Add lettuce leaves, tomato slices, cucumber slices, and pickles if using.
4. **Top and Serve:**
   - Place the second slice of bread on top, condiment side facing the filling.
   - Garnish with fresh herbs if desired, then cut the sandwich in half if preferred.

## Serving Suggestions:

- Serve with a side of chips, fresh fruit, or a simple salad.
- Pair with a light beverage or a cold drink.

**Kanapka z Wędliną** is a delicious and easy-to-make sandwich that's perfect for a quick lunch or snack. Enjoy!

**Żurek z Kiełbasą (Sour Rye Soup with Sausage)**

**Ingredients:**

- 1 cup sour rye starter (żur) or 2 cups prepared żurek mix
- 1 lb (450 g) Polish sausage (kiełbasa), sliced
- 1 medium onion, chopped
- 2 cloves garlic, minced
- 2 bay leaves
- 1 tsp dried marjoram
- 4 cups (1 liter) beef or vegetable broth
- 2 medium potatoes, peeled and diced
- 1-2 tbsp vegetable oil
- Salt and pepper to taste
- 1/4 cup (60 ml) heavy cream (optional)
- 4 slices of bread (optional, for serving)

**Instructions:**

1. **Cook the Sausage:**
    - In a large pot, heat vegetable oil over medium heat.
    - Add chopped onion and cook until translucent, about 5 minutes.
    - Add minced garlic and cook for an additional minute.
    - Add sliced sausage and cook for 5-7 minutes, allowing it to brown slightly.
2. **Prepare the Soup Base:**
    - Add diced potatoes, bay leaves, and dried marjoram to the pot.
    - Pour in the beef or vegetable broth and bring to a boil. Reduce heat and simmer until potatoes are tender, about 10-15 minutes.
3. **Add the Sour Rye:**
    - Stir in the sour rye starter (żur) or prepared żurek mix. Simmer for an additional 5 minutes. Adjust seasoning with salt and pepper to taste.
4. **Finish the Soup:**
    - If using, stir in heavy cream for a richer texture.
    - Simmer for a few more minutes, then remove bay leaves.
5. **Serve:**
    - Serve hot, with slices of bread on the side if desired.

## Serving Suggestions:

- Garnish with fresh parsley or dill if desired.
- Enjoy with a side of pickles or a light salad.

**Żurek z Kiełbasą** is a hearty and flavorful soup that's perfect for a comforting meal.

**Kanapka z Sałatką (Salad Sandwich)**

**Ingredients:**

- **For the Egg Salad:**
    - 4 large eggs
    - 2 tbsp mayonnaise
    - 1 tsp Dijon mustard
    - 1 tbsp fresh chives or dill, chopped (optional)
    - Salt and pepper to taste
- **For the Sandwich:**
    - 4 slices of bread (white, whole wheat, or rye)
    - Lettuce leaves (optional)
    - Tomato slices (optional)
    - Pickles or gherkins (optional)

**Instructions:**

1. **Prepare the Egg Salad:**
    - Hard-boil the eggs: Place eggs in a saucepan and cover with water. Bring to a boil, then reduce heat and simmer for 9-12 minutes. Cool in an ice bath and peel.
    - Chop the eggs and place them in a bowl.
    - Add mayonnaise, Dijon mustard, chopped chives or dill if using, salt, and pepper. Mix until well combined.
2. **Prepare the Bread:**
    - If desired, lightly toast the bread slices.
3. **Assemble the Sandwich:**
    - Spread a layer of egg salad on one slice of bread.
    - Add lettuce leaves, tomato slices, or pickles if desired.
    - Top with another slice of bread.
4. **Serve:**
    - Cut the sandwich in half if preferred and serve immediately.

## Variations:

- **Chicken Salad:** Use cooked, shredded chicken mixed with mayonnaise, celery, and herbs.
- **Tuna Salad:** Combine canned tuna with mayonnaise, chopped celery, and a squeeze of lemon juice.
- **Vegetable Salad:** Use a mix of finely chopped vegetables with a light vinaigrette or creamy dressing.

## Serving Suggestions:

- Enjoy with a side of fresh fruit, chips, or a simple green salad.

- Pair with a light beverage or a cup of tea.

**Kanapka z Sałatką** is a flexible and easy-to-make sandwich that can be customized with your favorite salad filling. Enjoy!

**Kiełbasa w Musztardzie (Sausage with Mustard)**

**Ingredients:**

- 1 lb (450 g) Polish sausage (kielbasa) or your favorite sausage
- 1-2 tbsp mustard (yellow, Dijon, or your preferred type)
- 1 tbsp vegetable oil (optional, for grilling or frying)
- 1 small onion, sliced (optional, for sautéing)
- Fresh parsley or dill (for garnish, optional)

**Instructions:**

1. **Cook the Sausage:**
    - **Grilling:** Preheat your grill to medium-high heat. Grill the sausages for 5-7 minutes on each side, or until cooked through and nicely charred.
    - **Pan-Frying:** Heat vegetable oil in a skillet over medium heat. Add sausages and cook for 5-7 minutes on each side, or until browned and cooked through.
    - **Boiling:** Alternatively, you can simmer the sausages in a pot of water for 15-20 minutes until cooked.
2. **Prepare the Mustard:**
    - Place mustard in a small bowl or serving dish. You can use a single type of mustard or mix different varieties to taste.
3. **Optional - Sauté the Onions:**
    - If you like, sauté the onion slices in a skillet with a bit of oil until they are caramelized, about 10 minutes. This adds a sweet and savory element to the dish.
4. **Serve:**
    - Slice the cooked sausages and arrange them on a plate.
    - Serve with mustard on the side for dipping.
    - Garnish with fresh parsley or dill if desired.

## Serving Suggestions:

- Serve with crusty bread, pickles, or sauerkraut for a traditional touch.
- Enjoy with a side of potato salad or coleslaw.

**Kiełbasa w Musztardzie** is a simple yet satisfying dish that highlights the robust flavor of sausages paired with the tanginess of mustard. It's perfect for a quick meal or as a hearty snack. Enjoy!

# Kanapka z Pstrągiem w Sosie (Trout Sandwich in Sauce)

**Ingredients:**

- **For the Trout:**
    - 2 trout fillets (about 6 oz/170 g each)
    - 1 tbsp olive oil
    - 1 lemon, juiced
    - Salt and pepper to taste
    - 1 tsp dried dill or fresh dill (optional)
- **For the Sauce:**
    - 1/4 cup (60 ml) sour cream or heavy cream
    - 1 tbsp mayonnaise
    - 1 tsp Dijon mustard
    - 1 tbsp fresh dill or parsley, chopped
    - 1 clove garlic, minced
    - Salt and pepper to taste
- **For the Sandwich:**
    - 4 slices of bread (white, whole wheat, or rye)
    - Lettuce leaves
    - Tomato slices
    - Cucumber slices (optional)

**Instructions:**

1. **Prepare the Trout:**
    - Preheat your oven to 375°F (190°C).
    - Season trout fillets with salt, pepper, and dill if using. Drizzle with lemon juice.
    - Heat olive oil in a skillet over medium heat. Sear the trout fillets, skin-side down, for 2-3 minutes until crispy.
    - Transfer to the oven and bake for 5-7 minutes, or until the trout is cooked through and flakes easily with a fork. Let cool slightly, then flake the fish into bite-sized pieces.
2. **Make the Sauce:**
    - In a small bowl, combine sour cream or heavy cream, mayonnaise, Dijon mustard, fresh dill or parsley, minced garlic, salt, and pepper. Mix well.
3. **Prepare the Bread:**
    - If desired, lightly toast the bread slices.
4. **Assemble the Sandwich:**
    - Spread a generous amount of the sauce on one side of each bread slice.
    - Layer lettuce leaves, trout pieces, tomato slices, and cucumber slices if using on one slice of bread.
    - Top with the second slice of bread, sauce side down.
5. **Serve:**
    - Cut the sandwich in half if desired and serve immediately.

**Serving Suggestions:**

- Serve with a side of chips, a fresh salad, or pickles.
- Enjoy with a light beverage or a cold drink.

**Kanapka z Pstrągiem w Sosie** is a flavorful and satisfying sandwich that combines tender trout with a creamy, tangy sauce. Enjoy this elegant yet simple meal!

**Kotlet Po Wiedeńsku (Viennese Cutlet)**

**Ingredients:**

- 4 veal or pork cutlets (about 6 oz/170 g each), pounded thin
- 1 cup all-purpose flour
- 2 large eggs
- 1 cup breadcrumbs (preferably fresh)
- 1/2 cup vegetable oil or clarified butter, for frying
- Salt and pepper to taste
- Lemon wedges, for serving
- Fresh parsley (optional, for garnish)

**Instructions:**

1. **Prepare the Cutlets:**
    - Place each cutlet between two pieces of plastic wrap or parchment paper.
    - Using a meat mallet or rolling pin, pound the cutlets until they are about 1/4 inch (0.5 cm) thick. This helps tenderize the meat and ensures even cooking.
    - Season both sides of the cutlets with salt and pepper.
2. **Bread the Cutlets:**
    - Set up a breading station with three shallow dishes:
        - In the first dish, place the flour.
        - In the second dish, beat the eggs with a pinch of salt.
        - In the third dish, place the breadcrumbs.
    - Dredge each cutlet in flour, shaking off excess.
    - Dip in the beaten eggs, allowing excess to drip off.
    - Coat thoroughly with breadcrumbs, pressing lightly to adhere.
3. **Fry the Cutlets:**
    - Heat vegetable oil or clarified butter in a large skillet over medium-high heat.
    - Fry the cutlets for about 3-4 minutes on each side, or until golden brown and cooked through. Avoid overcrowding the pan; cook in batches if necessary.
    - Transfer the cooked cutlets to a paper towel-lined plate to drain excess oil.
4. **Serve:**
    - Arrange the cutlets on a serving platter.
    - Garnish with fresh parsley if desired and serve with lemon wedges.

## Serving Suggestions:

- Accompany with potato salad, mashed potatoes, or a simple green salad.
- Serve with a side of pickles or sauerkraut for added flavor.

**Kotlet Po Wiedeńsku** is a crispy and flavorful dish that's perfect for a hearty meal. Enjoy the classic taste of this beloved cutlet!

# Kanapka z Rillettes (Pork Rillettes Sandwich)

**Ingredients:**

- **For the Pork Rillettes:**
    - 1 lb (450 g) pork shoulder, cut into chunks
    - 1/2 lb (225 g) pork belly, cut into chunks
    - 1 small onion, chopped
    - 2 cloves garlic, minced
    - 1 bay leaf
    - 1 tsp dried thyme
    - 1/2 cup (120 ml) white wine or chicken broth
    - 1/2 tsp salt
    - 1/4 tsp black pepper
    - 2 tbsp lard or vegetable oil (for cooking)
- **For the Sandwich:**
    - 4 slices of bread (baguette, ciabatta, or your choice)
    - 1-2 tbsp Dijon mustard or mayonnaise (optional)
    - Pickles or gherkins (optional, for added crunch)
    - Lettuce leaves (optional)

**Instructions:**

1. **Prepare the Rillettes:**
    - In a large heavy-bottomed pot or Dutch oven, heat lard or vegetable oil over medium heat.
    - Add the pork shoulder and pork belly chunks, and cook until browned on all sides, about 8-10 minutes.
    - Add chopped onion and minced garlic, and cook until softened, about 5 minutes.
    - Stir in the bay leaf, dried thyme, salt, and black pepper.
    - Pour in the white wine or chicken broth, and bring to a simmer.
    - Cover and cook on low heat for 2-3 hours, or until the pork is very tender and can be easily shredded with a fork.
2. **Shred and Cool:**
    - Remove the pork from the pot and shred it using two forks. Return the shredded pork to the pot and stir to combine with the cooking juices.
    - Allow the mixture to cool slightly. It will firm up as it cools.
3. **Assemble the Sandwich:**
    - If desired, spread Dijon mustard or mayonnaise on the slices of bread.
    - Generously spread the pork rillettes on one slice of bread.
    - Add pickles or gherkins and lettuce leaves if using.
4. **Top and Serve:**
    - Place the second slice of bread on top to complete the sandwich.
    - Cut in half if desired and serve immediately.

**Serving Suggestions:**

- Enjoy with a side of fresh fruit, chips, or a simple salad.
- Pair with a light beverage or a cold drink.

**Kanapka z Rillettes** offers a rich and savory experience with the creamy texture of the pork spread complemented by your choice of sandwich toppings. It's a delicious and satisfying option for any meal. Enjoy!

## Schab po Warszawsku (Warsaw-style Pork)

**Ingredients:**

- **For the Pork:**
    - 4 pork loin chops or pork tenderloin medallions (about 6 oz/170 g each)
    - 1 cup all-purpose flour
    - 2 large eggs
    - 1 cup breadcrumbs (preferably fresh)
    - 1/2 cup vegetable oil or clarified butter, for frying
    - Salt and pepper to taste
- **For the Sauce:**
    - 2 tbsp vegetable oil or butter
    - 1 medium onion, finely chopped
    - 1 clove garlic, minced
    - 1/2 cup (120 ml) white wine or chicken broth
    - 1 cup (240 ml) heavy cream
    - 1 tsp dried thyme or marjoram
    - Salt and pepper to taste

**Instructions:**

1. **Prepare the Pork:**
    - Place each pork chop or medallion between two sheets of plastic wrap or parchment paper.
    - Using a meat mallet or rolling pin, pound the pork to about 1/4 inch (0.5 cm) thickness.
    - Season both sides of the pork with salt and pepper.
2. **Bread the Pork:**
    - Set up a breading station with three shallow dishes:
        - In the first dish, place the flour.
        - In the second dish, beat the eggs with a pinch of salt.
        - In the third dish, place the breadcrumbs.
    - Dredge each piece of pork in flour, shaking off excess.
    - Dip in the beaten eggs, allowing excess to drip off.
    - Coat thoroughly with breadcrumbs, pressing lightly to adhere.
3. **Fry the Pork:**
    - Heat vegetable oil or clarified butter in a large skillet over medium-high heat.
    - Fry the pork chops or medallions for about 3-4 minutes on each side, or until golden brown and cooked through. Avoid overcrowding the pan; cook in batches if necessary.
    - Transfer the cooked pork to a paper towel-lined plate to drain excess oil.
4. **Prepare the Sauce:**
    - In the same skillet used for frying, add vegetable oil or butter if needed.
    - Sauté the chopped onion until translucent, about 5 minutes.

- Add minced garlic and cook for another minute.
- Deglaze the pan with white wine or chicken broth, scraping up any browned bits from the bottom.
- Stir in the heavy cream and dried thyme or marjoram. Simmer until the sauce thickens slightly, about 5 minutes.
- Season with salt and pepper to taste.

5. **Serve:**
   - Spoon the sauce over the fried pork.
   - Serve hot with your choice of sides, such as mashed potatoes, rice, or steamed vegetables.

## Serving Suggestions:

- **Mashed Potatoes**: Classic and creamy, perfect for soaking up the sauce.
- **Rice**: Simple and versatile, complements the pork well.
- **Steamed Vegetables**: Adds a fresh and healthy balance to the meal.

**Schab po Warszawsku** is a flavorful and comforting dish that combines crispy pork with a rich, creamy sauce. Enjoy this traditional Polish favorite!

**Kanapka z Kapustą (Cabbage Sandwich)**

**Ingredients:**

- **For the Sautéed Cabbage:**
    - 2 cups shredded cabbage (green or red)
    - 1 medium onion, thinly sliced
    - 2 tbsp vegetable oil or butter
    - 1 tbsp apple cider vinegar or lemon juice
    - Salt and pepper to taste
    - 1/2 tsp caraway seeds or cumin (optional)
- **For the Sandwich:**
    - 4 slices of bread (rye, whole wheat, or your choice)
    - 2 tbsp mayonnaise or mustard (optional)
    - Pickles or gherkins (optional)
    - Fresh herbs (e.g., parsley or dill, optional)

**Instructions:**

1. **Prepare the Sautéed Cabbage:**
    - Heat vegetable oil or butter in a large skillet over medium heat.
    - Add sliced onion and cook until translucent, about 5 minutes.
    - Add shredded cabbage and cook, stirring occasionally, until the cabbage is tender and slightly caramelized, about 10-15 minutes.
    - Stir in apple cider vinegar or lemon juice, salt, pepper, and caraway seeds or cumin if using. Cook for another 2-3 minutes. Adjust seasoning to taste.
2. **Prepare the Bread:**
    - If desired, lightly toast the bread slices.
3. **Assemble the Sandwich:**
    - Spread mayonnaise or mustard on one side of each bread slice if using.
    - Layer the sautéed cabbage mixture on one slice of bread.
    - Add pickles or gherkins and fresh herbs if desired.
4. **Top and Serve:**
    - Place the second slice of bread on top, condiment side down.
    - Cut the sandwich in half if preferred and serve immediately.

## Serving Suggestions:

- **Simple Side Salad**: A light salad adds freshness.
- **Soup**: Pair with a bowl of soup for a complete meal.

**Kanapka z Kapustą** offers a savory and satisfying flavor with the tenderness of sautéed cabbage. Enjoy this comforting and easy-to-make sandwich!

**Sernik na Zimno (Cold Cheesecake)**

**Ingredients:**

- **For the Crust:**
    - 200 g (7 oz) digestive biscuits or graham crackers, crushed
    - 100 g (1/2 cup) melted butter or margarine
- **For the Filling:**
    - 500 g (18 oz) cream cheese (or curd cheese, if available), softened
    - 200 ml (7 fl oz) heavy cream
    - 150 g (3/4 cup) powdered sugar
    - 1 tsp vanilla extract
    - 2 tbsp lemon juice (or to taste)
    - 2 tbsp gelatin powder
    - 1/4 cup (60 ml) water (for dissolving gelatin)
- **For the Topping (optional):**
    - Fresh fruit, fruit compote, or fruit jelly

**Instructions:**

1. **Prepare the Crust:**
    - In a bowl, mix the crushed biscuits with melted butter until combined.
    - Press the mixture into the bottom of a springform pan or pie dish to form an even layer.
    - Refrigerate while preparing the filling.
2. **Prepare the Filling:**
    - Dissolve the gelatin powder in 1/4 cup of water and let it sit for 5 minutes. Then, heat gently until the gelatin is fully dissolved (do not boil).
    - In a large bowl, beat the softened cream cheese until smooth.
    - Add powdered sugar, vanilla extract, and lemon juice. Mix well.
    - In a separate bowl, whip the heavy cream until stiff peaks form.
    - Gently fold the whipped cream into the cream cheese mixture.
    - Gradually fold in the dissolved gelatin until well combined.
3. **Assemble the Cheesecake:**
    - Pour the filling over the chilled crust in the springform pan or pie dish.
    - Smooth the top with a spatula and refrigerate for at least 4 hours, or until set.
4. **Add Topping and Serve:**
    - Once the cheesecake is set, top with fresh fruit, fruit compote, or fruit jelly if desired.
    - Release the cheesecake from the springform pan and transfer to a serving plate.

## Serving Suggestions:

- **With a Fruit Sauce**: A berry or citrus sauce adds extra flavor.
- **With Whipped Cream**: For added richness, serve with a dollop of whipped cream.

**Sernik na Zimno** is a delicious and refreshing dessert that's perfect for any occasion. Enjoy this classic Polish treat!

**Kanapka z Wątróbką (Liver Sandwich)**

**Ingredients:**

- **For the Liver Pâté:**
    - 500 g (1 lb) chicken liver or pork liver, cleaned and trimmed
    - 1 medium onion, chopped
    - 2 cloves garlic, minced
    - 2 tbsp butter or oil
    - 1/2 cup (120 ml) heavy cream
    - 1/4 cup (60 ml) chicken broth (or more if needed)
    - 1/4 tsp dried thyme or sage
    - Salt and pepper to taste
- **For the Sandwich:**
    - 4 slices of bread (rye, whole wheat, or your choice)
    - Pickles or gherkins (optional)
    - Fresh herbs (e.g., parsley, optional)

**Instructions:**

1. **Prepare the Liver Pâté:**
    - Heat butter or oil in a skillet over medium heat. Add chopped onion and cook until softened, about 5 minutes.
    - Add minced garlic and cook for another minute.
    - Increase heat to medium-high and add liver. Cook until browned on the outside but still pink in the center, about 5-7 minutes.
    - Transfer liver, onion, and garlic to a food processor. Add heavy cream, chicken broth, dried thyme or sage, salt, and pepper.
    - Process until smooth. If the pâté is too thick, add more chicken broth to reach desired consistency.
    - Taste and adjust seasoning if necessary. Let cool to room temperature.
2. **Prepare the Bread:**
    - If desired, lightly toast the bread slices.
3. **Assemble the Sandwich:**
    - Spread a generous layer of liver pâté on one slice of bread.
    - Add pickles or gherkins and fresh herbs if desired.
4. **Top and Serve:**
    - Place the second slice of bread on top, and cut the sandwich in half if preferred.
    - Serve immediately or refrigerate until ready to eat.

## Serving Suggestions:

- **With Pickles**: Adds a tangy contrast to the rich pâté.
- **With a Side Salad**: Complements the sandwich with freshness.

**Kanapka z Wątróbką** offers a rich and savory flavor with the smoothness of liver pâté. Enjoy this classic and satisfying sandwich!

**Placki z Kurczaka (Chicken Pancakes)**

**Ingredients:**

- **For the Chicken Pancakes:**
    - 500 g (1 lb) ground chicken or finely chopped chicken breast
    - 1 small onion, finely chopped
    - 1 egg
    - 1/2 cup (60 g) breadcrumbs or flour (for binding)
    - 1/4 cup (60 ml) milk
    - 2 tbsp fresh parsley or dill, chopped
    - 1 garlic clove, minced
    - 1/2 tsp paprika
    - 1/4 tsp ground black pepper
    - Salt to taste
    - Vegetable oil, for frying
- **For Serving (optional):**
    - Sour cream or Greek yogurt
    - Fresh herbs
    - Lemon wedges or a side salad

**Instructions:**

1. **Prepare the Mixture:**
    - In a large bowl, combine the ground chicken, finely chopped onion, egg, breadcrumbs or flour, milk, fresh herbs, minced garlic, paprika, black pepper, and salt.
    - Mix until all ingredients are well combined. The mixture should be moist but firm enough to hold together when formed into pancakes. If it's too loose, add a bit more breadcrumbs or flour.
2. **Shape and Cook:**
    - Heat a few tablespoons of vegetable oil in a large skillet over medium heat.
    - Take a spoonful of the chicken mixture and shape it into a patty or pancake, about 1/2 inch thick.
    - Fry the pancakes in batches, cooking each side for about 3-4 minutes, or until golden brown and cooked through. The internal temperature should reach 165°F (74°C).
3. **Drain and Serve:**
    - Transfer the cooked pancakes to a paper towel-lined plate to drain excess oil.
    - Serve hot with a dollop of sour cream or Greek yogurt, fresh herbs, and lemon wedges or a side salad if desired.

## Serving Suggestions:

- **With a Fresh Salad**: A light, crunchy salad complements the richness of the chicken pancakes.
- **With Mashed Potatoes or Rice**: For a more substantial meal.

**Placki z Kurczaka** are versatile and flavorful, making them a great choice for a quick meal or a tasty snack. Enjoy these crispy, golden pancakes!

**Kanapka z Krewetkami (Shrimp Sandwich)**

**Ingredients:**

- **For the Shrimp Filling:**
    - 250 g (1/2 lb) cooked shrimp, peeled and deveined
    - 2 tbsp mayonnaise
    - 1 tbsp Dijon mustard
    - 1 tbsp lemon juice
    - 1 tbsp fresh dill or parsley, chopped
    - 1 small celery stalk, finely diced
    - 1 small red onion, finely diced
    - 1 clove garlic, minced (optional)
    - Salt and pepper to taste
- **For the Sandwich:**
    - 4 slices of bread (white, whole wheat, or your choice)
    - Lettuce leaves
    - Tomato slices (optional)
    - Cucumber slices (optional)
    - Pickles or gherkins (optional)

**Instructions:**

1. **Prepare the Shrimp Filling:**
    - Chop the cooked shrimp into bite-sized pieces.
    - In a medium bowl, combine mayonnaise, Dijon mustard, lemon juice, and fresh dill or parsley.
    - Add the chopped shrimp, diced celery, diced red onion, and minced garlic if using. Mix until well combined.
    - Season with salt and pepper to taste. Chill in the refrigerator for at least 30 minutes to let the flavors meld.
2. **Prepare the Bread:**
    - If desired, lightly toast the bread slices.
3. **Assemble the Sandwich:**
    - Place a layer of lettuce leaves on one slice of bread.
    - Spoon the shrimp filling over the lettuce.
    - Add tomato slices, cucumber slices, and pickles or gherkins if desired.
    - Top with the second slice of bread.
4. **Serve:**
    - Cut the sandwich in half if desired and serve immediately.

## Serving Suggestions:

- **With a Side Salad**: A fresh green salad complements the sandwich well.
- **With Chips**: Adds a crunchy texture to your meal.

**Kanapka z Krewetkami** is a versatile and elegant sandwich that can be customized with your favorite ingredients. Enjoy this refreshing and tasty treat!

**Zupa Pomidorowa z Chlebem (Tomato Soup with Bread)**

**Ingredients:**

- **For the Tomato Soup:**
    - 2 tbsp olive oil
    - 1 medium onion, chopped
    - 2 cloves garlic, minced
    - 1 can (400 g/14 oz) crushed tomatoes
    - 2 cups (480 ml) vegetable or chicken broth
    - 1 tsp dried basil or oregano
    - 1/2 tsp sugar (optional, to balance acidity)
    - Salt and pepper to taste
    - 1/4 cup (60 ml) heavy cream (optional, for creamier texture)
    - Fresh basil or parsley, for garnish (optional)
- **For Serving:**
    - Fresh crusty bread (e.g., baguette, sourdough, or rye)
    - Optional: Grated cheese for topping (e.g., Parmesan or mozzarella)

**Instructions:**

1. **Prepare the Soup:**
    - Heat olive oil in a large pot over medium heat. Add chopped onion and cook until softened, about 5 minutes.
    - Add minced garlic and cook for another minute.
    - Stir in crushed tomatoes and vegetable or chicken broth. Bring to a simmer.
    - Add dried basil or oregano and sugar if using. Season with salt and pepper to taste.
    - Simmer for 15-20 minutes, allowing flavors to meld. For a smoother texture, use an immersion blender to puree the soup or carefully transfer to a blender in batches.
    - If desired, stir in heavy cream for a richer soup. Heat through.
2. **Prepare the Bread:**
    - Slice the bread and toast if desired. You can also serve it fresh.
3. **Serve:**
    - Ladle the hot tomato soup into bowls.
    - Garnish with fresh basil or parsley and a sprinkle of grated cheese if using.
    - Serve with slices of crusty bread on the side.

## Serving Suggestions:

- **With a Side Salad**: A simple green salad adds freshness.
- **With Cheese Toast**: Adds extra flavor and makes the meal more substantial.

**Zupa Pomidorowa z Chlebem** offers a hearty and satisfying meal with the rich flavors of tomato soup paired with comforting bread. Enjoy this classic Polish combination!

**Kanapka z Pstrągiem w Bułce (Trout in Bread)**

**Ingredients:**

- **For the Trout:**
    - 2 trout fillets, skinless and boneless
    - 2 tbsp olive oil
    - 1 lemon, sliced
    - 1 tsp dried dill or fresh dill, chopped
    - Salt and pepper to taste
- **For the Sandwich:**
    - 4 bread rolls or buns (e.g., ciabatta, baguette, or your choice)
    - 2 tbsp mayonnaise or Greek yogurt
    - 1 tbsp Dijon mustard (optional)
    - Lettuce leaves
    - Sliced tomato (optional)
    - Sliced cucumber (optional)
    - Fresh dill or parsley for garnish (optional)

**Instructions:**

1. **Prepare the Trout:**
    - Preheat the oven to 375°F (190°C).
    - Place the trout fillets on a baking sheet. Drizzle with olive oil and season with salt, pepper, and dried dill.
    - Top with lemon slices.
    - Bake for 12-15 minutes, or until the trout is cooked through and flakes easily with a fork.
2. **Prepare the Bread Rolls:**
    - Slice the bread rolls or buns in half if they are not already pre-sliced.
    - If desired, lightly toast the bread rolls in a toaster or oven for extra crunch.
3. **Assemble the Sandwich:**
    - Spread mayonnaise or Greek yogurt on the inside of each bread roll. Add Dijon mustard if using.
    - Place a layer of lettuce leaves on the bottom half of each roll.
    - Flake the cooked trout and arrange it on top of the lettuce.
    - Add sliced tomato and cucumber if desired.
    - Garnish with fresh dill or parsley if using.
4. **Top and Serve:**
    - Place the top half of the bread roll on the filled bottom half.
    - Serve immediately or wrap in paper for a portable meal.

## Serving Suggestions:

- **With a Side Salad**: Complements the freshness of the sandwich.

- **With Chips**: Adds a crunchy texture to the meal.

**Kanapka z Pstrągiem w Bułce** offers a light and tasty option with the delicate flavor of trout. Enjoy this simple yet delicious sandwich!

# Kotlet w Bułce (Cutlet in Bread)

**Ingredients:**

- **For the Cutlet:**
    - 4 pork cutlets or chicken breasts (about 1/2 inch thick)
    - 1 cup all-purpose flour
    - 2 large eggs, beaten
    - 1 cup breadcrumbs
    - Salt and pepper to taste
    - Vegetable oil, for frying
- **For the Sandwich:**
    - 4 bread rolls or buns (e.g., ciabatta, kaiser rolls, or your choice)
    - 4 tbsp mayonnaise or mustard
    - Lettuce leaves
    - Sliced tomato
    - Sliced cucumber (optional)
    - Pickles or gherkins (optional)
    - Fresh parsley or dill (optional)

**Instructions:**

1. **Prepare the Cutlets:**
    - Place each cutlet between two sheets of plastic wrap and gently pound with a meat mallet to an even thickness.
    - Season both sides with salt and pepper.
    - Set up a breading station with three shallow dishes:
        - In the first dish, place the flour.
        - In the second dish, beat the eggs.
        - In the third dish, place the breadcrumbs.
    - Dredge each cutlet in flour, dip in beaten eggs, and coat with breadcrumbs.
    - Heat vegetable oil in a large skillet over medium-high heat.
    - Fry the cutlets for 3-4 minutes per side, or until golden brown and cooked through. Drain on paper towels.
2. **Prepare the Bread Rolls:**
    - If desired, lightly toast the bread rolls.
3. **Assemble the Sandwich:**
    - Spread mayonnaise or mustard on the inside of each bread roll.
    - Place a lettuce leaf on the bottom half of each roll.
    - Add a fried cutlet on top of the lettuce.
    - Top with sliced tomato, cucumber, and pickles if desired.
    - Garnish with fresh parsley or dill if using.
4. **Serve:**
    - Place the top half of the bread roll on the filled bottom half.
    - Serve immediately or wrap for a portable meal.

**Serving Suggestions:**

- **With a Side Salad**: Adds freshness to balance the richness of the cutlet.
- **With Fries or Chips**: Completes the meal with a crunchy side.

**Kotlet w Bułce** is a comforting and satisfying sandwich that combines crispy cutlets with fresh and flavorful toppings. Enjoy this classic treat!

**Kanapka z Tuńczykiem (Tuna Sandwich)**

**Ingredients:**

- **For the Tuna Filling:**
    - 1 can (185 g/6.5 oz) tuna in oil or water, drained
    - 2 tbsp mayonnaise
    - 1 tbsp Dijon mustard (optional)
    - 1 small celery stalk, finely diced
    - 1 small red onion, finely diced
    - 1 tbsp fresh parsley or dill, chopped
    - 1 tbsp lemon juice
    - Salt and pepper to taste
- **For the Sandwich:**
    - 4 slices of bread (white, whole wheat, or your choice)
    - Lettuce leaves
    - Sliced tomato (optional)
    - Sliced cucumber (optional)
    - Pickles or gherkins (optional)

**Instructions:**

1. **Prepare the Tuna Filling:**
    - In a medium bowl, combine the drained tuna, mayonnaise, Dijon mustard (if using), diced celery, diced red onion, fresh parsley or dill, and lemon juice.
    - Mix until well combined. Season with salt and pepper to taste.
2. **Prepare the Bread:**
    - If desired, lightly toast the bread slices.
3. **Assemble the Sandwich:**
    - Place a layer of lettuce leaves on one slice of bread.
    - Spoon a generous amount of tuna filling over the lettuce.
    - Add sliced tomato, cucumber, and pickles or gherkins if desired.
    - Top with the second slice of bread.
4. **Serve:**
    - Cut the sandwich in half if desired and serve immediately.

## Serving Suggestions:

- **With a Side Salad**: Complements the sandwich with freshness.
- **With Chips**: Adds a crunchy texture to your meal.

**Kanapka z Tuńczykiem** is a quick and satisfying sandwich that's perfect for lunch or a light meal. Enjoy this classic and tasty option!

**Ziemniaki z Boczkiem (Potatoes with Bacon)**

**Ingredients:**

- **For the Dish:**
    - 600 g (1.3 lbs) potatoes, peeled and diced
    - 200 g (7 oz) bacon, diced
    - 1 medium onion, chopped
    - 2 cloves garlic, minced
    - 2 tbsp vegetable oil or butter
    - 1 tsp dried thyme or rosemary (optional)
    - Salt and pepper to taste
    - Fresh parsley, chopped (for garnish)

**Instructions:**

1. **Prepare the Potatoes:**
    - Bring a pot of salted water to a boil. Add diced potatoes and cook until just tender, about 10 minutes. Drain and set aside.
2. **Cook the Bacon:**
    - In a large skillet, cook diced bacon over medium heat until crispy, about 5-7 minutes. Remove the bacon with a slotted spoon and set aside, leaving some bacon fat in the skillet.
3. **Sauté the Onion and Garlic:**
    - In the same skillet with the bacon fat, add chopped onion and cook until softened, about 5 minutes.
    - Add minced garlic and cook for another minute.
4. **Cook the Potatoes:**
    - Add vegetable oil or butter to the skillet if needed. Add the cooked potatoes to the skillet and cook, stirring occasionally, until they are golden and crispy, about 10 minutes.
    - Stir in the cooked bacon and season with dried thyme or rosemary if using, salt, and pepper.
5. **Serve:**
    - Garnish with fresh parsley and serve hot.

## Serving Suggestions:

- **As a Side Dish**: Pairs well with grilled meats or a simple salad.
- **As a Main Course**: Add a side of steamed vegetables for a complete meal.

**Ziemniaki z Boczkiem** is a comforting and satisfying dish with the rich flavor of bacon and crispy potatoes. Enjoy this delicious recipe!

**Kanapka z Mieszanką Wędlin (Mixed Cold Cuts Sandwich)**

**Ingredients:**

- **For the Sandwich:**
    - 4 slices of bread (e.g., rye, whole wheat, ciabatta, or your choice)
    - 4-6 varieties of cold cuts (such as ham, salami, turkey, roast beef, or pastrami), thinly sliced
    - 2-4 slices of cheese (such as Swiss, cheddar, or provolone)
    - Lettuce leaves
    - Sliced tomato
    - Sliced cucumber
    - Pickles or gherkins
    - Mayonnaise or mustard
    - Optional: Sliced onions or olives

**Instructions:**

1. **Prepare the Bread:**
    - If desired, lightly toast the bread slices.
2. **Assemble the Sandwich:**
    - Spread mayonnaise or mustard on one side of each slice of bread.
    - Layer the cold cuts on one slice of bread, starting with the thicker slices and alternating types to create a varied texture and flavor.
    - Place a slice of cheese on top of the cold cuts.
    - Add lettuce leaves, sliced tomato, and cucumber.
    - Include pickles or gherkins and any optional ingredients like sliced onions or olives.
3. **Top and Serve:**
    - Place the second slice of bread on top of the filled ingredients.
    - Cut the sandwich in half if desired.

## Serving Suggestions:

- **With a Side Salad**: A light salad complements the richness of the cold cuts.
- **With Chips or Fries**: Adds a crunchy side to your meal.

**Kanapka z Mieszanką Wędlin** is a delicious and customizable sandwich that showcases a variety of cold cuts. Enjoy creating your own mix of flavors and textures with this classic and satisfying option!

**Schab z Kością (Bone-in Pork Cutlet)**

**Ingredients:**

- 4 bone-in pork chops (about 1-inch thick)
- 2 tbsp olive oil or vegetable oil
- 1 tbsp butter
- 2 cloves garlic, minced
- 1 tsp dried thyme or rosemary
- Salt and pepper to taste
- Optional: 1/2 cup (120 ml) chicken broth or white wine (for deglazing)
- Fresh parsley, chopped (for garnish)

**Instructions:**

1. **Prepare the Pork Chops:**
   - Pat the pork chops dry with paper towels.
   - Season both sides generously with salt, pepper, and dried thyme or rosemary.
2. **Cook the Pork Chops:**
   - Heat olive oil and butter in a large skillet over medium-high heat.
   - Add the pork chops and cook for 4-5 minutes per side, or until the internal temperature reaches 145°F (63°C) and the chops are golden brown and cooked through. Adjust cooking time depending on thickness.
3. **Optional: Make a Pan Sauce:**
   - Remove the pork chops from the skillet and set aside to rest.
   - In the same skillet, add minced garlic and cook for about 30 seconds, until fragrant.
   - Deglaze the pan with chicken broth or white wine, scraping up any browned bits from the bottom of the pan. Let it simmer for a few minutes to reduce slightly.
4. **Serve:**
   - Serve the pork chops hot, garnished with fresh parsley if desired.
   - Spoon any pan sauce over the chops if made.

## Serving Suggestions:

- **With Mashed Potatoes**: Complements the rich flavor of the pork.
- **With Steamed Vegetables**: Adds freshness and balance.

**Schab z Kością** is a robust and satisfying dish that's perfect for a hearty meal. Enjoy this classic pork cutlet with your favorite sides!

**Kanapka z Kiełbasą Wieprzową (Pork Sausage Sandwich)**

**Ingredients:**

- **For the Sandwich:**
    - 4 pork sausages (e.g., Polish kielbasa or your choice), grilled or pan-fried
    - 4 bread rolls or buns (e.g., ciabatta, baguette, or your choice)
    - 1 tbsp mustard or mayonnaise
    - Sliced onions (raw or caramelized)
    - Sliced pickles or gherkins
    - Lettuce leaves
    - Optional: Sliced tomato, sauerkraut, or cheese

**Instructions:**

1. **Cook the Sausages:**
    - Grill or pan-fry the pork sausages according to package instructions until fully cooked and nicely browned. Set aside.
2. **Prepare the Bread Rolls:**
    - If desired, lightly toast the bread rolls.
3. **Assemble the Sandwich:**
    - Spread mustard or mayonnaise on the inside of each bread roll.
    - Place a cooked sausage on the bottom half of each roll.
    - Add sliced onions, pickles, and any optional ingredients like tomato slices, sauerkraut, or cheese.
    - Top with lettuce leaves.
4. **Serve:**
    - Place the top half of the bread roll on the filled bottom half.
    - Serve immediately.

## Serving Suggestions:

- **With a Side Salad**: Adds freshness to the meal.
- **With Potato Chips**: Provides a crunchy side.

**Kanapka z Kiełbasą Wieprzową** is a flavorful and satisfying sandwich, perfect for a quick meal or casual gathering. Enjoy this hearty treat!

**Wątróbka w Śmietanie (Liver in Cream)**

**Ingredients:**

- 500 g (1 lb) chicken liver or beef liver, cleaned and trimmed
- 2 tbsp vegetable oil or butter
- 1 medium onion, finely chopped
- 2 cloves garlic, minced
- 1/2 cup (120 ml) heavy cream
- 1/4 cup (60 ml) chicken broth or water
- 1 tsp dried thyme or rosemary
- Salt and pepper to taste
- Fresh parsley, chopped (for garnish)

**Instructions:**

1. **Prepare the Liver:**
   - Rinse the liver under cold water and pat dry with paper towels. Remove any connective tissue or membranes.
   - Cut the liver into bite-sized pieces.
2. **Cook the Liver:**
   - Heat oil or butter in a large skillet over medium heat.
   - Add chopped onion and cook until softened, about 5 minutes.
   - Add minced garlic and cook for another minute.
   - Increase heat to medium-high and add the liver pieces. Cook until browned on all sides, about 4-5 minutes.
3. **Make the Cream Sauce:**
   - Reduce heat to medium and pour in the heavy cream and chicken broth. Stir to combine.
   - Add dried thyme or rosemary, salt, and pepper.
   - Simmer for 5-7 minutes, or until the liver is cooked through and the sauce has thickened.
4. **Serve:**
   - Garnish with fresh parsley and serve hot.

## Serving Suggestions:

- **With Mashed Potatoes**: Complements the creamy sauce.
- **With Bread**: Ideal for soaking up the sauce.

**Wątróbka w Śmietanie** offers a rich and savory flavor, making it a comforting and satisfying dish. Enjoy this classic Polish recipe!

**Kanapka z Pieczonym Kurczakiem (Roast Chicken Sandwich)**

**Ingredients:**

- **For the Sandwich:**
    - 2 cups cooked, shredded roast chicken (from a rotisserie chicken or homemade)
    - 4 slices of bread (e.g., whole wheat, sourdough, or ciabatta) or 4 rolls
    - 2 tbsp mayonnaise or Greek yogurt
    - 1 tbsp Dijon mustard (optional)
    - Lettuce leaves
    - Sliced tomato
    - Sliced cucumber (optional)
    - Pickles or gherkins (optional)
    - Fresh herbs like parsley or dill (optional, for garnish)

**Instructions:**

1. **Prepare the Chicken:**
    - If using a rotisserie chicken, remove the meat from the bones and shred it into bite-sized pieces.
    - If using homemade roast chicken, shred or chop the cooked chicken.
2. **Make the Chicken Mixture:**
    - In a bowl, mix the shredded chicken with mayonnaise or Greek yogurt. Add Dijon mustard if using.
    - Season with salt and pepper to taste. Stir until well combined.
3. **Prepare the Bread:**
    - If desired, lightly toast the bread slices or rolls.
4. **Assemble the Sandwich:**
    - Spread mayonnaise or mustard on the inside of each bread slice or roll.
    - Place a layer of lettuce leaves on the bottom half of each bread slice or roll.
    - Spoon a generous amount of the chicken mixture over the lettuce.
    - Add sliced tomato, cucumber, and pickles or gherkins if desired.
    - Garnish with fresh herbs if using.
5. **Top and Serve:**
    - Place the top half of the bread slice or roll on the filled bottom half.
    - Cut the sandwich in half if desired and serve immediately.

## Serving Suggestions:

- **With a Side Salad**: Complements the freshness of the sandwich.
- **With Chips or Fries**: Adds a crunchy or hearty side.

**Kanapka z Pieczonym Kurczakiem** is a versatile and satisfying sandwich that's perfect for lunch or a casual meal. Enjoy this easy and flavorful option!

**Placki Ziemniaczane z Wędliną (Potato Pancakes with Cold Cuts)**

**Ingredients:**

- **For the Potato Pancakes:**
    - 4 medium potatoes, peeled and grated
    - 1 small onion, finely grated
    - 1 egg
    - 2-3 tbsp all-purpose flour
    - Salt and pepper to taste
    - Vegetable oil, for frying
- **For the Topping:**
    - 200 g (7 oz) cold cuts (e.g., ham, salami, or any preferred variety), sliced
    - 1/2 cup sour cream or Greek yogurt
    - Fresh chives or parsley, chopped (for garnish)

**Instructions:**

1. **Prepare the Potato Pancakes:**
    - Place the grated potatoes and onion in a clean cloth or paper towel and squeeze out excess moisture.
    - In a large bowl, mix the grated potatoes and onion with the egg, flour, salt, and pepper until well combined.
    - Heat vegetable oil in a large skillet over medium-high heat.
    - Drop spoonfuls of the potato mixture into the skillet and flatten slightly with the back of the spoon. Fry until golden brown and crispy, about 3-4 minutes per side.
    - Remove and drain on paper towels.
2. **Prepare the Topping:**
    - Arrange the cold cuts on a plate or serving platter.
3. **Assemble and Serve:**
    - Serve the hot potato pancakes with cold cuts on the side.
    - Top each pancake with a dollop of sour cream or Greek yogurt.
    - Garnish with fresh chives or parsley.

## Serving Suggestions:

- **With Pickles or Gherkins**: Adds a tangy contrast to the richness.
- **With a Simple Salad**: Provides freshness and balance.

**Placki Ziemniaczane z Wędliną** offers a delightful combination of crispy, savory pancakes and flavorful cold cuts, making it a hearty and satisfying dish. Enjoy this classic recipe!

**Kanapka z Fasolką (Bean Sandwich)**

**Ingredients:**

- **For the Bean Filling:**
    - 1 can (400 g/14 oz) beans (e.g., white beans, kidney beans, or black beans), drained and rinsed
    - 2 tbsp olive oil
    - 1 small onion, finely chopped
    - 1 garlic clove, minced
    - 1/2 tsp dried thyme or rosemary
    - 1 tbsp lemon juice
    - Salt and pepper to taste
- **For the Sandwich:**
    - 4 slices of bread (e.g., whole wheat, sourdough, or ciabatta)
    - 1-2 tbsp mayonnaise or hummus
    - Lettuce leaves
    - Sliced tomato
    - Sliced cucumber (optional)
    - Pickles or gherkins (optional)

**Instructions:**

1. **Prepare the Bean Filling:**
    - Heat olive oil in a skillet over medium heat.
    - Add chopped onion and cook until softened, about 5 minutes.
    - Add minced garlic and cook for another minute.
    - Add the beans, dried thyme or rosemary, lemon juice, salt, and pepper. Cook for 5-7 minutes, stirring occasionally, until the beans are heated through and slightly mashed. Adjust seasoning as needed.
2. **Prepare the Bread:**
    - If desired, lightly toast the bread slices.
3. **Assemble the Sandwich:**
    - Spread mayonnaise or hummus on one side of each bread slice.
    - Place a layer of lettuce leaves on the bottom half of each slice.
    - Spoon a generous amount of the bean mixture over the lettuce.
    - Add sliced tomato, cucumber, and pickles or gherkins if desired.
    - Top with the second slice of bread.
4. **Serve:**
    - Cut the sandwich in half if desired and serve immediately.

## Serving Suggestions:

- **With a Side Salad**: Complements the beans with freshness.
- **With Crispy Chips**: Adds a crunchy side to the meal.

**Kanapka z Fasolką** is a hearty and nutritious option that's easy to prepare. Enjoy this versatile and tasty sandwich!

www.ingramcontent.com/pod-product-compliance
Lightning Source LLC
LaVergne TN
LVHW061947070526
838199LV00060B/4020